P9-AQD-517

Girl's
Handbook to
Growing Up

Girl's
Handbook to
Growing Up

Anita Ganeri

For Helen, love AG.

With thanks to Kath Cook and to all those friends
with puberty-aged daughters who offered invaluable advice.

First published in 2011, by Scholastic Children's Books
Euston House, 24 Eversholt Street,
London NW1 1DB, UK

A division of Scholastic Ltd
www.scholastic.com
London ~ New York ~ Toronto ~ Sydney ~ Auckland
Mexico City ~ New Delhi ~ Hong Kong

ISBN 978-1-4351-5028-7

Manufactured in Singapore
Lot #
2 4 6 8 10 9 7 5 3 1
08/13

CONTENTS

GROWING UP

From the minute you're born, you start growing and changing, though you don't notice it much at first. In just a few years you go from being a baby to a toddler to a child, and through all sorts of stages in between.

But from the age of about nine or ten you start to change in a big way, and fast. You might have noticed some of these changes already. You get taller and wider. Your breasts get bigger and feel tender. You feel perfectly fine one minute, then dead moody the next. DON'T PANIC – there's nothing wrong with you. You're not turning into a completely different person or an alien from Planet Weird. You're growing up! It's perfectly normal and natural. And it happens to everyone. The changes that you are experiencing are called puberty. And the chances are, if you're reading this *Smart Girl's Guide*, they're happening to you.

WHAT IS PUBERTY?

Puberty marks a brand-new phase in your life. It's when your body changes from a child's body to an adult's. And all of this gets you ready for having babies one day, if you want them. Puberty can be exciting, scary, worrying and confusing, all at the same time. But it's also nothing to worry about. And you'll soon get used to it ... honestly!

WHY DOES IT HAPPEN?

Puberty happens because powerful chemicals, called hormones, whizz around your body in your bloodstream. You've got lots of different hormones and each type carries a different message to a different part of your body. Some hormones tell your body to start growing (and also when to stop). Some hormones control how your body uses up energy. And some hormones, especially sex hormones, prepare your body for being an adult, and that's when puberty starts...

HORMONES: THE INSIDE STORY

1. Welcome to your busy brain! A bit of your brain, the hypothalamus, sends a hormone message to another bit of your brain, the pituitary gland.

2. This tells the pituitary gland that it's time to make two new types of hormones – FSH and LH.

3. The FSH and LH pour into your bloodstream and are carried to your ovaries (they're your sex organs, in the lower part of your abdomen).

4. Now your ovaries start churning out sex hormones (the main types are called oestrogen and progesterone).

5. And it's these hormones that set off the big changes that happen to you during puberty.

WHEN DOES IT HAPPEN?

Exactly when and how these changes start depends on lots of different things. For most girls, puberty starts at around 10 or 11 years old. But it can happen at any time between the ages of 8 and 13 – there's no set age. You might feel embarrassed or worried if you start puberty early or late, and you're out of step with your friends. But rememember, everyone is different. It really doesn't matter if you start your periods before your friends, or if you're the last one to need to wear a bra. There's nothing wrong with you! When you start puberty makes no difference at all.

WHAT HAPPENS NEXT?

So what actually happens when puberty kicks in? The main thing is that your body changes, both on the inside and the outside. Here's a list of some of the tell-tale signs you might notice. It looks like a very long list but don't worry – they don't all start at once. Puberty doesn't happen overnight – it can take a few years. Luckily.

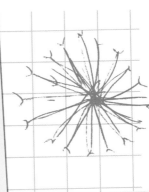

FACT FILE: PUBERTY

On the outside...
- You grow taller and more quickly than in the past.
- Your body shape changes; your hips get wider.
- Your breasts begin to develop and grow bigger.
- Your pubic hair starts growing.

- You grow hair under your arms and on your legs.
- You might start getting pimples on your face and body.
- Your hair might get greasier than normal.

On the inside...
- Your sex organs develop inside your body.
- Your periods start.

FUNNY FEELINGS

Puberty isn't just about how your body changes physically. It can cause chaos with your feelings and moods! One minute you're feeling fabulous; the next, you've got serious ATTITUDE. ←

Like the physical changes, your see-sawing emotions are all part of the growing-up process. And, again, your high-speed hormones are to blame. These mixed feelings can be strange and worrying, but as your hormones settle down, so will they.

For many smart girls, puberty can be an exciting time. But it can also be a difficult one. For starters, you have to cope with your body changing, just when you're feeling most self-conscious about how you look. If you're worried about anything that's happening to you, talk to someone about it. If you can't face talking to your parents, try your big sister, a teacher, an aunt or the school nurse.

BOY TALK

Boys also go through puberty, and their bodies change too. Some changes are like those that happen to girls. Boys grow taller, get pimples and grow more hair on their bodies. Their sex organs, called testicles, develop and start making sex hormones (such as testosterone). Other changes only happen to boys. For example, their voices "break" and can suddenly sound squeaky while they are talking, like a bunch of chipmunks. Eventually their voices settle down and sound deeper all the time.

ABOUT THIS BOOK

This book will help you to find out the facts about puberty so that you've got a better idea of what to expect. Knowing what's happening to your body will help to make puberty a lot less worrying and confusing. When you've finished reading this book, be smart and pass it on to your parents or guardians. Then they'll know what you're going through. Smart!

BODY TALK

During puberty your body changes on the outside and the inside. The external changes are easy to see, though they don't all happen at once. Big changes also occur inside you, as your sex organs start growing and developing. These changes are all kicked off by your sex hormones (see pages 9 and 20). Ready to check out the changes? Let's start with your body shape...

ALL GROWN UP

One of the first changes you'll notice is getting taller. And the weird thing is that it happens so suddenly and you'll constantly have people telling you how much you've grown. During puberty you grow faster than at any other time in your life, apart from when you're a baby, and it's called a growth spurt. You usually grow fastest between the ages of 12 and 13 – maybe even by as much as 4 inches in a year – but some girls start earlier or later. This growth spurt lasts for around two to three years. You should almost have finished growing by the time you're 15. And by the time you're 18, you'll be at your adult height.

THE "RIGHT" HEIGHT?

You and your friends are probably always moaning that you're too short or too tall. If you're tall, you'd love to be shorter. If you're short, you've always wanted to be tall. There's no such thing as a "right" height for anyone, and you can't do much about how tall or short you are. This is because your height, and lots of your other features, such as eye color and body shape, are fixed by your genes. These are special codes in the cells of your body that are passed on to you by your parents. Chances are if both of your parents are tall, you'll be tall, too. And if they're short, you'll be short. That's just how it is.

Smart Girl Talk

The sleeves on your favorite top are suddenly way too short. Don't panic! It's only because, during your growth spurt, the fastest-growing bits of you are your arms and legs. It's nothing to worry about, though it might feel a bit weird while you wait for the rest of your body to catch up.

CHANGING SHAPE

Before puberty, girls and boys have pretty similar body shapes. But all of this changes as your sex hormones set to work. Soon after girls start getting taller, their hips and waist get wider and curvier, and they put on weight. Some girls get curvier than others – it depends on your natural body shape. And the weight gain is supposed to happen so you definitely DON'T NEED to go on a diet. Like everything else, these changes are preparing your body for having babies one day, and are normal parts of growing up.

Smart Girl Talk

During your growth spurt, your arms and legs might start aching. These "growing pains" can be a real pain, but they don't last for long and shouldn't need any special treatment. You'll usually find that they go away on their own, but a massage or heat pad can help. Or ask your parents for a mild painkiller.

HAIR AWARE

Another change that's hard to miss is your body becoming hairier. You'll spot hair sprouting in places where you didn't have hair before. First, the hair on your arms and legs gets darker. (The hair on your top lip might get darker too.) Then hair grows in a triangle in your groin. It's called pubic hair, and it's different from the hair on your head. It's wiry and curly, and it never grows very long. About a year after your pubic hair grows, you also get hair in your armpits. No one's exactly sure what pubic and armpit hair is for. Some animals use the smell of sweat to attract a mate, though this doesn't happen with humans. It sounds gross, so no wonder.

SURVIVAL TIP

The hair on your body is completely natural but if it bothers you, there are lots of ways to get rid of it. Best to tell your mom if you're trying any of these. She can help you follow the instructions and do it properly.

SHAVING

Using a razor is quite quick and easy for hair on your legs and armpits, but be careful. Always use a clean razor and sensitive-skin shaving foam. Afterwards, pat your skin with a cool, damp flannel. If your skin feels sore, your razor may be blunt. Don't use a deodorant straight after shaving your armpits – it'll sting like mad. And don't try shaving on your own the first time, just in case you cut yourself.

HAIR-REMOVAL CREAM

Spread the cream on your skin, leave it for a while, then wash it off. It contains chemicals that dissolve hairs at their roots. Make sure you test the cream on a small patch of skin first – it can really irritate your skin. And follow the instructions carefully.

WAXING

Waxing uses strips of soft wax to pull hairs out. It works well but can be quite painful, like ripping off a bandage! You can buy waxing kits to use at home, but it's better to get it done in a proper salon, though it's likely to cost more.

PLUCKING

Plucking with tweezers is a smart way of getting rid of single hairs — in your eyebrows for example. But it's not much good for larger areas of hair, like on your legs. Buy a good pair of tweezers, and don't prod or poke your skin too much or it will get red and sore.

EPILATING

An epilator is a hand-held gadget a bit like an electric razor. It has rotating blades that grab hold of hairs and tweak them out. It's easy to do, lasts a long time and doesn't make a mess, though it can be a bit painful. Put moisturizer on afterwards to soothe your skin.

BUDDING BREASTS

Some girls can't wait for them to grow and look forward to wearing a bra. Others dread the whole thing. Mostly it's a case of mixed feelings – you love and hate them at the same time. Yep, we're talking about breasts – an obvious sign that your body is changing. But what are breasts, how do they grow, and what are they for? Check out our breast-owner's guide...

① The first thing you notice is your nipples starting to stick out from your chest.

② Then a small bump grows behind each nipple. This is called a breast bud.

③ Your breasts start to fill out as fat fills the space around the nipples. The fat gives them their size and shape.

④ Your nipples, and the circles of skin around them (called the areolae), get bigger and darker.

⑤ At first, your breasts are pointy but they soon become rounder and fuller.

BREAST BUSINESS:
AGONY AUNT

Q: All my friends wear bras. Why haven't my breasts started growing yet?

A: Don't worry. Everyone develops at different times. Breasts can start growing as early as eight years old, or as late as 13. Your breasts may carry on growing until you're about 17 or 18, and they can get bigger and smaller throughout your life, too.

Q: Help! One of my breasts is bigger than the other. Am I normal?

A: Totally! Often one breast grows faster than the other, at least to start with. They even out eventually, though very few people have breasts of exactly equal size. Many girls worry about their breasts and think that they should be bigger or smaller. But breasts come in all shapes and sizes.

Q: Why don't boys grow breasts? And what are they for anyway?

A: Breasts are mainly for making milk for feeding babies. That's why boys don't have them. The parts of a breast that make milk are deep inside, under a cushion of fat. But they don't make milk until a woman has a baby. Then the milk squirts out through tiny holes in the nipples.

Q: Why are my breasts so painful?

A: When your breasts start growing, they can feel tingly and sore. This is nothing to worry about and it will soon wear off. They might also ache a bit before you have a period. This can carry on beyond puberty too.

Q: When do I need to start wearing a bra?

A: It's really up to you! You don't have to wear a bra at all, if you don't want to. But if your breasts are quite large and heavy, a bra will help to support them and make you feel more comfortable. It's a good idea to wear a special, extra-supportive sports bra if you're doing sports. And if you just can't wait, there are also bras for very small breasts.

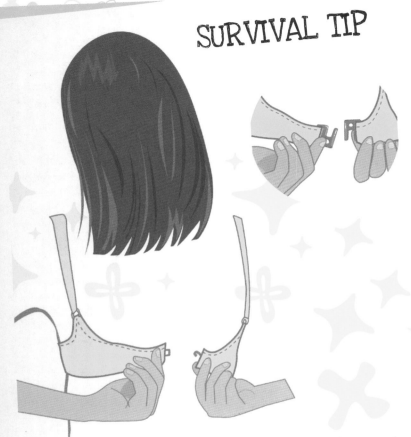

It can take a while to get used to wearing a bra, and you might find yourself constantly fiddling with it. You have to get used to fastening and adjusting it, and making sure that the straps don't keep falling off your shoulders or dig in. So it's really worthwhile making certain that you wear the right size bra to start off with.

BRA-BUYING GUIDE

Buying your first bra is a big deal, but there are plenty of people around to help. If you feel nervous, take your mom, big sister or a friend shopping with you. Otherwise, the shop assistants will happily help measure you. If you're doing this bit yourself, here's how to measure up...

1. Measure just below your breasts and around your ribcage and back. Keep the tape measure fairly tight so it doesn't sag. Add 5 inches to the measurement. This is your chest size. (If your chest measurement's an odd number, round it up.)

2. Now measure around your body, across the fullest part of your breasts. Be careful not to pull the tape measure too tight so it flattens them. Subtract your chest measurement from this measurement. This is your cup size.

- AA cup: the two measurements are the same
- A cup: there's a ½ inch difference
- B cup: there's a 1 inch difference
- C cup: there's a 2 inch difference
- D cup: there's a 3 inch difference

3. Your chest and cup sizes combined give your bra size. So you could be a 32AA or a 34B, and so on. You need to get both sizes right to make sure your bra really fits.

Smart Girl Talk

Now you've got your measurements, you can buy your bra! There are lots of different types to choose from. Try a few on to see which style and color you like the best. Put your top back on over each bra to check the bra fits well.

CHANGING ON THE INSIDE

While all of these changes are happening on the outside of your body, there are plenty of changes going on inside you too. Your sex organs (or "reproductive" organs) are growing and developing so you can have babies one day, if you want them. And even though you can't see these organs, it's useful to know where they are and what they do.

Smart Girl Talk

To make a baby, a sperm from a man's body has to join with an egg inside a woman. This may happen when a man and woman have sex (or sexual intercourse). During sex, the man's penis fits inside the woman's vagina and a fluid, containing sperm, squirts out. If a sperm meets an egg, it may be fertilized, and a baby may start growing. Then the woman is pregnant. But people don't only have sex to make babies. It's also a way of showing they love each other and can make them feel good. If they don't want to have a baby, they can use contraceptives such as condoms, that stop a woman from getting pregnant.

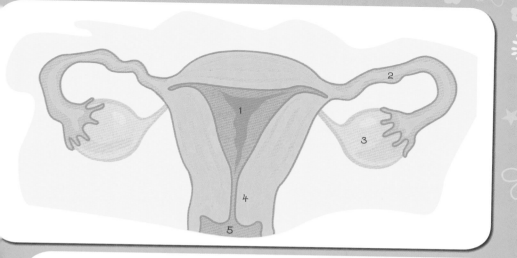

1 Uterus (womb): This is where a baby grows if you have one. It's normally the size and shape of a pear. But it's made of strong muscle and stretches as the baby grows.

2 Fallopian tubes: They're tubes that connect your ovaries to your uterus (womb). The eggs from your ovaries travel along them.

3 Ovaries: Two small organs where your eggs are stored. Each ovary is the size and shape of a walnut and contains hundreds of thousands of eggs.

4 Cervix (neck of the womb): A narrow passageway that connects the uterus to the vagina.

5 Vagina: The passage leading from the uterus to the outside of your body. Its walls are made of stretchy muscle.

The vulva or genitals are on the outside of your body. They're mostly hidden by your pubic hair.

- Clitoris: A pea-shaped bump that's very sensitive to touch.
- Labia (inner and outer): Folds of skin that close around the genitals to protect them.
- Vaginal opening: The stretchy opening to the vagina.

PERIOD PUZZLE

Starting your periods is one of the most important changes that happens to you during puberty. Each month you'll have a few days of bleeding from your vagina – a sign that your body's really growing up. Sure, it sounds a bit scary, but don't worry. Periods show that your body – and your hormones – are working properly. Some girls feel shy or embarrassed about their periods, or wish that they didn't happen at all. Other girls feel nervous about starting and wonder how they'll cope. After all, this is a big event in your life. But if you're clued up about what's happening, you'll find periods much easier to manage.

PERIODS: THE INSIDE STORY

1. Each month a ripe egg pushes out of one of the ovaries and travels down a fallopian tube. This is called ovulation.

2. The egg travels along the fallopian tube until it reaches the uterus (womb).

3. Meanwhile, the uterus grows a thick, spongy lining of blood vessels. This is to make it a soft, safe place for a baby to grow, if th egg meets a sperm and is fertilized.

4. If the egg isn't fertilized, it breaks up and dissolves. Because the uterus lining isn't needed either, it also breaks up. Then it comes of the vagina as blood.

5. Your period has started! It's also called menstruating. But peop often call periods their "time of the month".

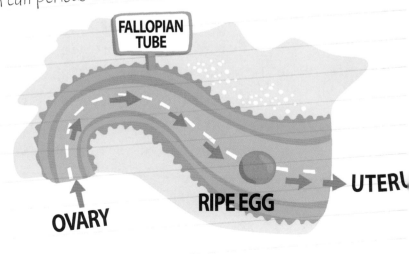

FALLOPIAN TUBE

OVARY

RIPE EGG

UTERU

WHEN DO PERIODS START?

Most girls start their periods around the age of 12 or 13. But everyone's different, and you could be as young as 8 years old or as old as 16. It seems that girls often start their periods at about the same time as their moms did. This is usually a year or two after your breasts have started growing, so that's another clue. Women carry on having periods until they are about 50 years old. Then periods become less and less regular, before eventually stopping altogether.

When you have a period, the first thing you might notice is some blood as you wipe yourself after going to the toilet. But you may get other clues for a day or two beforehand. Your breasts might feel sore and you might get backaches. You might also need to go to the toilet more often, and feel more tired and irritable than usual. All of these things should clear up once your period actually starts.

Smart Girl Talk

If you notice a white or yellowish stain in your pants, don't panic! It's nothing to be embarrassed about. It's caused by a mucus~like fluid that leaks out from your vagina. The fluid is called vaginal discharge and it helps to keep your vagina healthy. You get more just before your periods start. If the discharge is thick or itchy or smelly, you might have an infection, called thrush. You can get a cream for it from the drugstore.

HOW OFTEN DO PERIODS HAPPEN?

```
         1  2  3  4  5
 6  7  8  9 10 11 12
13 14 15 16 17 18 19
20 21 22 23 24 25 26
27 28 29 30 31
```

```
         1  2  3  4  5
 6  7  8  9 10 11 12
13 14 15 16 17 18 19
20 21 22 23 24 25 26
27 28 29 30 31
```

Periods happen once a month, or about every 28 days. This is called your monthly or menstrual cycle. But the length of your cycle can vary a lot, from as short as 21 days to as long as 35 days, or even longer. For the first year or so, though, you may find that your periods don't follow a regular cycle. You could have a period, then not have another one for a couple of months. Once things settle down, it's a good idea to make a note of when your next period is due. Count the first day of your period as Day 1. Then you can be sure to have pads (see page 40) or tampons (see page 42) handy when your period starts.

A period usually lasts for around five days, but it may be shorter or longer. And it may change from month to month, and from person to person. The bleeding is likely to be heavier (more blood) during the first few days, then get lighter (less blood) later on. Or it might start off light, become heavier, then get lighter again.

PERIOD PAINS AND PMS

At the start of your period, you might get aching, dragging cramps called "period" pains. They usually only last for a day or two and are quite mild. If they get worse, try doing some gentle exercise such as walking. It's probably the last thing you feel like but it can help a lot. You could also try relaxing in a hot bath, or lying down with a hot-water bottle on your tummy. If these don't work, ask your mom or dad if you can have a painkiller.

But there's another big period pain... A day or two before your period, you might feel tired and bloated, or extra grumpy and snappy. Don't worry, you're not turning into a monster. It's something called pre-menstrual syndrome or PMS. "Pre-menstrual" means before your period. There's no magic cure but eating healthy food, taking exercise and getting plenty of sleep can help.

PERIOD PROTECTION

Having a period doesn't mean putting your life on hold. Actually, you can carry on pretty much as normal. You just need to be wearing the right sanitary protection to soak up the blood. Most smart girls choose towels (also called pads) or tampons, which you can buy from a drugstore or supermarket. There are lots of different kinds to choose from, so pick the type you feel most comfortable with, depending on how heavy or light your period is. Don't worry if it takes a few times to get this right.

FACT FILE:
SANITARY TOWELS

• Towels are rectangles of absorbent material that stick inside your pants. They soak up the blood as it comes out of your body.

• Change your towel every few hours, even if there's not much blood. If you're at school, break and lunch are good times to do this. This stops the pad from leaking and getting smelly. It also stops bacteria from building up and possibly causing an infection. If your period's heavy, change your towels more often.

• Most towels have sticky strips along them. You peel off the backing paper and stick the towel firmly in place to your pants. Other types also have sticky side flaps, called wings, which fold underneath your pants.

• Towels come in different sizes and thicknesses, to fit your shape and soak up different amounts of blood.

You might need a thicker towel at the beginning of your period, when the flow is heavier, and also at night, when you have to wear the same towel for longer. At other times, you should be able to use a thinner towel.

• Towels are easy and quick to use, especially when you first start your periods. The downside is that you can't go swimming if you're wearing them, and spares can be a bit bulky to carry around.

• Always get rid of towels carefully. Wrap a used towel in toilet paper or put it in a bag. Then put it in the trash. At school and in public toilets, there are often special bins for used towels and tampons, and there may be a supply of disposal bags too. Never flush towels down the toilet. They can block the pipes and are bad for the environment.

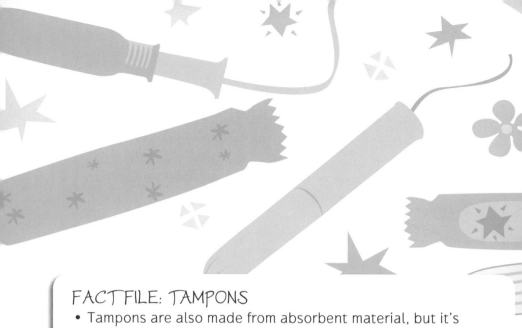

FACTFILE: TAMPONS

• Tampons are also made from absorbent material, but it's pressed into little rolls, about as long as your little finger. They have a piece of string attached to one end. They fit inside your body so they soak up blood before it flows out.

• You push the tampon into your vagina, leaving the string hanging out. Some tampons are covered in plastic wrapping. Tear this off and push the tampon inside you with your fingers. (Don't forget to wash your hands before and afterwards.) Others come inside a cardboard or plastic tube, called an applicator. Slide the applicator upwards to push the tampon out and into your vagina. You can use whichever type you find easiest. You'll find leaflets giving more instructions inside the tampon boxes.

- Change your tampon regularly, every four to eight hours, even if the flow is light. Change it more often when your period's heavier. To take out a tampon, pull gently on the string. Make sure you wash your hands before and afterwards.
- Like towels, tampons come in different sizes, for example, mini, regular and super. Choose which size to use, depending on how heavy your period is. You may need different sizes for different days, but always use the smallest-sized tampon you can.
- The great thing about tampons is that you can't see them, apart from the string. And you can go swimming while you're wearing one. They're also easy to store in your bag. The downside is that they can be a tricky to use at first, until you get used to them.
- You can flush tampons down the toiletbut it's better for the environment if you don't. The best thing is to dispose of them in the same way as towels (see page 41).

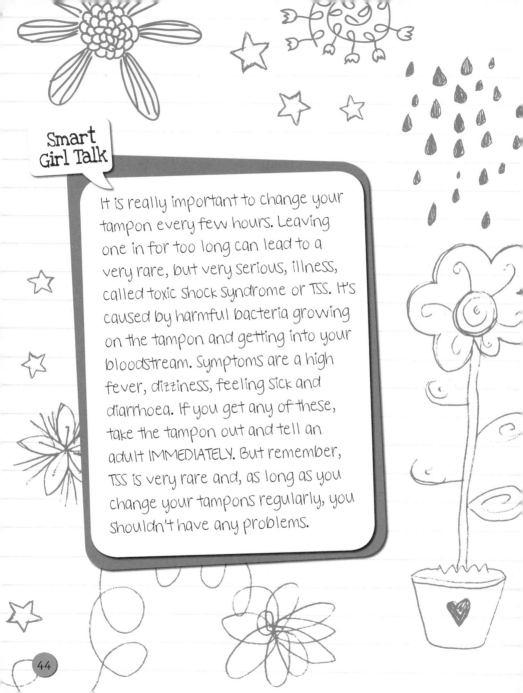

Smart Girl Talk

It is really important to change your tampon every few hours. Leaving one in for too long can lead to a very rare, but very serious, illness, called toxic shock syndrome or TSS. It's caused by harmful bacteria growing on the tampon and getting into your bloodstream. Symptoms are a high fever, dizziness, feeling sick and diarrhoea. If you get any of these, take the tampon out and tell an adult IMMEDIATELY. But remember, TSS is very rare and, as long as you change your tampons regularly, you shouldn't have any problems.

PERIOD PROBLEMS: AGONY AUNT

Q: Are towels or tampons best to start with?

A: It's really up to you. Many girls wear towels at first, until they're used to having periods. But you can wear tampons even if you've just started, and they're better for swimming and other sports. Some girls switch between the two, using pads at night and tampons during the day. It can help to talk to your mom or another adult about which is right for you.

Q: Can people tell if I'm wearing a pad?

A: In the bad old days (ask your gran!), pads were big, thick things that you wore pinned to a string-like belt with your pants on top. Yeuch! Today, you can get pads that are so thin, no one will ever know you're wearing them.

Q: Does it hurt to put tampons in and take them out?

A: No, it doesn't, though it's a good idea to try a tampon for the first time on a day when your period's quite heavy. It'll slip inside more easily. Try to relax as much as you can so that your muscles don't tense up. And if you can't do it the first time, leave it for a while and try again later.

Q: Could a tampon get lost inside me?

A: A tampon lies inside your vagina but it can't go any further up, into your womb, because your cervix (the neck of your womb) is too small. So it can't get lost inside you because there's nowhere for it to go. Sometimes the string can get tucked up inside but you just need to feel around and gently pull it out again.

Q: Is it true that blood comes gushing out?

A: No. Don't worry. The blood actually leaks out quite slowly. It won't suddenly come pouring out. And you only lose a small amount of blood – usually about two tablespoons – even though it might seem like a lot.

Q: What if blood leaks on to my clothes?

A: If you change your towel or tampon regularly, this shouldn't happen. If it does, and you can't get changed straightaway, tie your sweater or jacket around your waist so that no one can see the stain. Change your towel or tampon so it doesn't leak any more. To be on the safe side, some people like to wear dark-colored clothes during their periods. Some girls use tampons and pads together for added protection.

Q: What happens if I get my period at school?

A: It's a good idea to keep a supply of towels or tampons in your school bag or locker. Then you'll always be prepared. Otherwise, ask a teacher or the school nurse – they'll be able to help. In an emergency, fold some toilet paper, tissue paper or paper towels into a pad and tuck it into your pants.

STAYING HEALTHY

Growing up can be very hard work. Your body's changing so much, and so fast, it needs loads of energy to keep it going. Besides, there's all the energy you spend getting used to the new you. Sounds exhausting. But you'll find puberty a whole lot easier if you look after yourself. That means eating a healthy diet, keeping fit, getting plenty of sleep, and keeping clean. The good news is that it's easier to do this than you might think.

FACT FILE:
HEALTHY EATING

• You grow so fast during puberty that you need to eat around 2,200 calories a day. That's about as much food as an adult woman needs to eat.

• Eat at least five portions of fruit and veggies every day, even if you do nothing else on the healthy list. And if you get bored with apples and carrots, check out the supermarket shelves. There are loads of different types of delicious fruit and veg you can try, such as mangoes and sugar-snap peas.

• About a third of what you eat each day should be carbohydrates (things like bread, potatoes, pasta and rice). They're the foods that give you energy.

• It's a good idea to have 2–3 portions of milk, cheese or yogurt each day. These foods contain calcium to make your bones and teeth strong.

• Eat sensible (that is, not huge) amounts of meat, fish, eggs, beans and nuts for protein. It's also important for growing. And oily fish, such as tuna or mackerel, are great brain foods!

- Don't eat too much fatty or sugary food. That includes sugary drinks.
- Stick to healthy snacks, like fruit, nuts or a small piece of cheese. They're much better for you than chocolate bars, cookies or chips, though you can still have these as treats.
- Don't ever skip breakfast! Your body uses up energy even while you're asleep and you need to top this up in the morning. Eating breakfast will also make you feel more awake and stop you feeling peckish until lunchtime.

- Freshly cooked food is much better for you than ready meals or junk food. These don't have much goodness in them and contain unhealthy amounts of sugar, salt and fat.
- Drink plenty of water, at least six glasses a day, and more if you're doing exercise. It keeps your body healthy and it's great for your skin.

During puberty you'll put on weight, especially on your stomach and hips. This helps your body cope with all the changes it's going through. It doesn't mean you're getting fat, and you don't need to go on a diet. In fact, diets can stop your body growing and developing properly. Not a smart thing to do at all. Of course, it's easy to compare yourself with a friend who's taller and thinner than you are. But there are lots of different body shapes, and you can weigh more or less than someone else, and still be perfectly healthy.

EATING DISORDERS

Some girls are so
worried about their
weight that they'll try almost
anything to change it. They are
sure life would be better, or they'd
be more popular, if they were thinner.
Most people feel like this at some time, but
worrying about your weight can get out of control. Then people begin to
have a problem with food and eating, which takes over their lives, and
makes them unhappy and unhealthy. This is called an eating disorder.
The most common types are:

• Anorexia nervosa
People don't eat enough, cutting down on food until they're literally
starving. Even then, they still think they're fat. Side effects include hair
loss, thinning bones, dry and brittle nails, and extra hair growing on
your body.

• Bulimia nervosa

People "binge" on food. This means that they eat a lot, fast. Then they make themselves vomit or take laxatives (a type of medicine that makes you go for a poo) to get rid of the food so they don't put on weight. And then they start all over again. Some people don't binge, but take laxatives or make themselves vomit to get rid of any food they eat. Their bodies don't get enough vitamins and minerals to stay healthy, and vomiting so often it makes their teeth rot.

• Obesity

People put on so much weight that it puts their health seriously at risk. It's caused by eating too much and not doing enough exercise. An obese person is more at risk of suffering serious diseases, such as heart disease, diabetes and high blood pressure.

Smart Girl Talk

Eating disorders are bad news. Some people get so ill that they end up in the hospital. Some have long-term health problems. Some even die. If you have any worries about yourself or a friend, don't ignore them. Tell an adult you can trust immediately. The sooner you or your friend gets proper help, the better your chances of recovering.

LOOKING AFTER YOUR TEETH

By the time you're about 12 or 13, you'll have your adult teeth. They have to last for the rest of your life so you need to take good care of them...

• Have regular check-ups at the dentist, twice a year. Apart from checking your teeth and gums, your dentist also makes sure that your mouth and tongue are healthy, and gives you advice on brushing and flossing.

• If you wear braces, clean them thoroughly after meals and before you go to bed. Food can easily get stuck in them, speeding up the rate it rots your teeth.

• Learn how to floss your teeth. Ask your parents or your dentist to show you the best way. The floss gets rid of tiny specks of food that your toothbrush can't reach. If you like, you can use special brushes, called interdental ("between your teeth") brushes, instead of floss.

• Brush your teeth thoroughly twice a day, after breakfast and before you go to bed. This gets rid of plaque, a clear film that sticks to your teeth and attracts bacteria and sugar. If these build up, they can cause holes in your teeth and make your gums sore and swollen.

MORE THIS WAY!

• Spend about three minutes brushing, making sure that you brush all of your teeth, including the backs and the biting surfaces.

• Change your toothbrush every three months. Otherwise, plaque and bacteria can build up on the bristles. Some toothbrushes have bristles that turn a different color when it's time for a change.

GET MOVING

It's official! Exercise is good for you – especially during puberty. It helps make your body stronger as it's growing up. It also strengthens your heart and lungs, helps you look good, feel good, sleep better and feel less stressed. What's not to like? Ideally, you need to be active for an hour, five days a week. This sounds like a lot, but walking to school, taking the dog for a walk, or dancing around in your bedroom all count.

It's important to choose a sport or activity that you like. That way, you're more likely to stick at it. So don't worry if you can't stand the thought of going to the gym or for a jog. Why not give ice-skating, football, swimming or a martial art, like karate, a try? Try lots of different things until you find something you enjoy – as long as it gets you moving, it's fine. And if you're tempted to give up, just give it one more chance. When you start to notice how good you feel, and look, you'll soon find that you're motivated.

SLEEP TIGHT

Are your parents always complaining that they can't get you out of bed? Guess what? It's not your fault! Growing up is a really tiring experience. You need plenty of time to rest and recover, and that means around ten hours' sleep a night. Sleep's also the time when your body releases a hormone that's vital for your growth spurt. Trouble is, during puberty your sleep patterns may go crazy. You'll find that you can easily stay awake until late at night. But you haven't got the energy to get up the next morning. This means that you're probably not getting enough sleep, and it can make you cranky, clumsy and unable to concentrate. Try heading for bed a bit earlier, especially if it's a school day the next day. And if you're having trouble nodding off, read for a while or have a warm bath before you go to bed.

WHAT'S A PIMPLE?

Nobody wants them, but most people get them anyway. We're talking about pimples! You look in the mirror and there's a great big, glowing red pimple on your chin. Pimples are also called acne or zits, but they all mean the same thing. And they always seem to pop up at the worst possible time, like when you're heading out to a party. So how can you stop yourself from getting pimples? And what do you do if you've already got one?

PIMPLE PROBLEMS: AGONY AUNT

Q: Have I got pimples because my skin's dirty?

A: No. Almost everyone gets pimples at some time, even if they've got clean skin. They're a normal part of growing up. Again, your hormones are to blame. During puberty glands in your skin start producing loads of oil, called sebum. The oil seeps on to your skin through tiny holes, called pores. It keeps your skin soft and supple, but too much can clog up the pores and cause pimples.

Q: Does eating chips give you pimples?

A: There's no evidence that eating greasy food, like chips, or sweet things, like chocolate, gives you pimples. The oil on your skin's different from the oil in food. But eating a healthy diet and drinking water can certainly help keep your skin looking good.

Q: I've got pimples on my face and chest. Is this normal?

A: Totally. Pimples usually appear on your face but you can also get them on your shoulders, upper back and chest because that's where most of the oil glands are. But the same applies to pimples wherever they are – keep your skin clean and don't pick them!

Q: I hate my pimples. How can I get rid of them?

A: Wash your face twice a day in warm water using a mild soap, cleanser or facial wash. Don't use a flannel or scrub your face – it'll irritate your skin. You can also buy pimple treatments from the drugstore. The good news is that pimples usually stop after puberty.

Q: My friend squeezes her pimples. Is that okay?

A: No, it's a really bad idea! The pimples are likely to last longer and she may be left with tiny scars. Don't be tempted to squeeze, pick or play with your pimples. The germs from your hands will just make them worse.

Q: Why is my hair really greasy too?

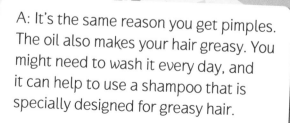

A: It's the same reason you get pimples. The oil also makes your hair greasy. You might need to wash it every day, and it can help to use a shampoo that is specially designed for greasy hair.

Smart Girl Talk

If you're worried about your pimples, tell an adult or your doctor. There are lots of creams, lotions and medicines that can help clear up your skin. Some girls find their pimples are worse in the days before their period. Stress also makes pimples worse so be smart and stay chilled.

NO SWEAT

When you hit puberty, you might need to wash more often than before. That's because you start to sweat a bit more. Everyone has sweat glands all over their bodies. And everybody sweats sometimes – it helps to cool your body down. This sweat is clear, watery and smell-free but if it mixes with bacteria on your skin, it can start to stink. This is called body odor, or BO. Trouble is, during puberty you start to make another kind of smellier sweat, especially under your arms and around your genitals. So it's doubly important to keep clean. Have a shower or bath every day, in the morning or before you go to bed, and after doing exercise. Wash your armpits, genitals, face and feet thoroughly. And change your clothes before they get smelly, especially your tops, socks and underwear.

Smart Girl Talk

Using a deodorant in your armpits can stop your sweat smelling. Deodorants are often combined with an antiperspirant that stops you sweating so much. You can choose from a roll-on or spray. Using one in the morning will help you stay fresh all day.

64

MIXED FEELINGS

Just as your hormones change your body physically, they can play tricks on your feelings, too. One minute you're on top of the world; the next, you're down in the dumps. Your moods swing so quickly, even you can't keep up.

You get upset more easily, and the tiniest things can trigger a major temper tantrum. You snap at everyone in sight, and get angry with your family and friends. You don't like it but you can't help it. What is going on? First of all, don't panic! You're not a nasty person and you don't have a bad life. Believe it or not, it really is normal to feel like this. Just ask your friends. Puberty's an exciting time but it's also when your feelings get more confused than ever before. The good news is that your hormones, and your feelings, will settle down eventually and you'll find it much easier to cope.

BEST FRIENDS; WORST ENEMIES

Friends are really important, for all sorts of reasons. You can have fun with them, share your problems with them, and in turn, look out for them if they're worried or upset. And some friendships can last your whole life. But friendships can also change during puberty. You might find yourself drifting away from the friends you had when you were younger, as you, and your interests, change. You might find your friendships change from day to day. One minute, you and your friend are never apart; the next, they, or you, have found a new best friend. And that's not all. You want to be one of the gang but you feel that you don't fit in, or that the others are deliberately leaving you out. It feels like the end of the world. But it doesn't usually take long before you're pals again, and have forgotten what all the fuss was about in the first place.

Smart Girl Talk

Making new friends can be tricky, especially if you've moved house or school. Joining something like an out-of-school club can help you to feel less lonely. But don't just sit in a corner, waiting for people to come and talk to you. Chances are they're feeling just as shy and nervous as you are. Take a deep breath and go and talk to someone. It can help to think of a question to ask, just to break the ice. And remember, even people who seem to have loads of friends are not always as smart or as self-confident as they look.

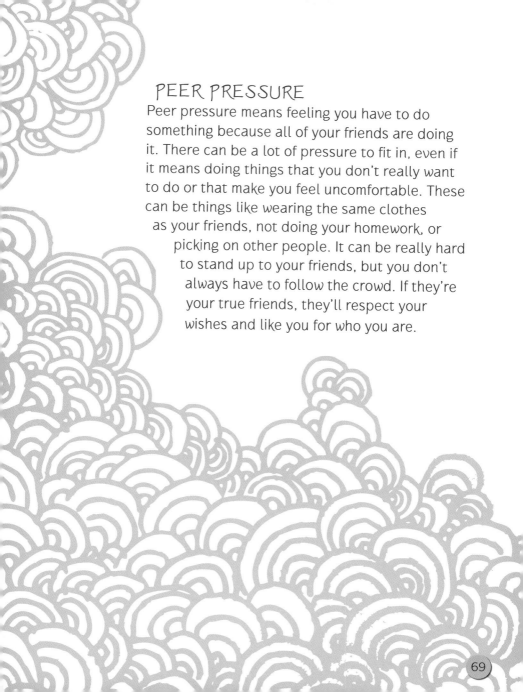

PEER PRESSURE

Peer pressure means feeling you have to do something because all of your friends are doing it. There can be a lot of pressure to fit in, even if it means doing things that you don't really want to do or that make you feel uncomfortable. These can be things like wearing the same clothes as your friends, not doing your homework, or picking on other people. It can be really hard to stand up to your friends, but you don't always have to follow the crowd. If they're your true friends, they'll respect your wishes and like you for who you are.

TROUBLE AT HOME

All families fall out sometimes but puberty's particularly tough. You're keen to act like an adult but sometimes you might think your parents are still treating you like a child. And you hate them for it (except you don't really). Trouble is, you're not grown up yet and your parents only want to keep you happy and safe. However annoying or embarrassing it is. Chances are, if you show they can trust you, they're much more likely to treat you as an adult. The smart thing to do is try seeing things from their point of view. If you understand why they're acting in a certain way, you might be able to reach a compromise ... and avoid a fight.

PARENT PROBLEMS: AGONY AUNT

Q: I came back late from my friend's house. And now my dad's grounded me.

A: He was probably really worried about where you were and if you were safe. If you want your parents to let you go out, make sure that you agree on a time you'll be back, then stick to it. If, for any reason, you're likely to be late, always let them know.

Q: I want some new sneakers but my parents won't give me the money.

A: If you want something expensive, like sneakers, why not volunteer to do some extra chores or contribute some of your pocket money? Your parents might agree to go halves with you. And they'll definitely appreciate that you understand the value of things.

Q: My parents are always moaning at me for being on the phone.

A: Well, they have to pay the phone bill! Again, you could offer to give them some of your pocket money. Or, if you've got a mobile phone, send texts – they're cheap or free.

Q: I borrowed my mom's top and forgot to put it back. She went ballistic.

A: How would you like it if she helped herself to your clothes? Just ask her next time – otherwise, you're likely to get the blame everytime something goes missing. Besides, if you respect her things, she's more likely to respect yours.

BOYS, BOYS, BOYS...

Puberty is also the time when you might start having exciting feelings you haven't had before. Up until now, boys were probably just friends, or not even friends, but suddenly you notice them in a different way. You might spot a particular person across the room, and get a strange, warm, fluttery feeling inside, quite different from anything you've ever felt. Before you know it, you've fallen in love! It's confusing, scary and exciting – all at the same time.

FACTFILE: CRAZY CRUSHES

Every time you see him, you get a funny feeling inside and your legs turn to jelly. You desperately want him to notice you, but you feel so flustered when he looks your way that you just want to run away and hide. Sounds like you've got a crush!

Even when he's not there, you think about him all the time, or spend hours writing his name over and over again. You try to find out everything you can about him, in the hope that you're the perfect match.

You can get crushes on anyone. It can be someone you know, like a classmate, a friend's older brother or a teacher. Or it can be someone like a famous sportsperson or film star that you're never even likely to meet.

If you have a crush on someone and he has a crush on you too, you feel on top of the world. Sadly, this isn't always the case. You might find out he doesn't feel the same way and it's heartbreaking. This is a very real and upsetting feeling but it will fade.

Crushes are hard work! They can hit you like a ton of bricks, and seem totally overwhelming at the time. But they don't usually last for longer than a few weeks, and are sometimes a lot shorter.

You might decide to tell your friends about your crush, or you might want to keep it a secret. But never tease someone because they've told you they've got a crush. After all, you wouldn't like it if they did that to you.

Of course, not all crushes are one-sided. The boy you like might just like you back! Before you know it, he's asked you out and you're going on a date. You're bound to feel nervous and it might help to go out with a group of friends. That way, you can get to know each other better without feeling under pressure. Smart!

Smart Girl Talk

Many girls get crushes on boys, but not everyone feels like that. When you're growing up, it's quite usual to like another girl, even if you go out with boys later. Some girls go on to date and have relationships with other women. They are known as lesbians.

BODY IMAGE

When you look in the mirror, what do you see? Are you shorter than you'd like to be? Do you want to be thinner, or have blue eyes instead of brown? How you think and feel about your body is called your body image. Some people are happy with how they look but many of us aren't. Trouble is, your body image is often very different from how you actually look. And during puberty this can be especially hard because your body's changing so much. Some times you might think you look fabulous. Other times you hate everything about yourself. You might feel doubly self-conscious about your body and think everyone's looking at you and making comments (which they are not!). It's normal to want to look good but it's also important to stay real. There can be a lot of pressure to look a certain way, but it's not worth trying to copy the celebrities you see in magazines and on TV. They only look that way because they spend a lot of time and money on their appearance. And the photos you see have most likely been deliberately altered to make them look better. In real life, people come in different shapes and sizes. It doesn't mean that you're not attractive or popular just because you're not tall and slim, with perfect teeth! So stop comparing yourself to other people, and learn to like the way you look.

Smart Girl Talk

There are ways of looking more confident, even if you're feeling like jelly. For starters, take a deep breath, put your shoulders back and stand up tall. You'll be amazed at how different you feel. Try not not fiddle with your hair or nibble your nails. If you're talking to someone, look them in the eye, not down or away from them. It seems scary at first, but practice makes perfect and it'll soon come naturally.

KEEPING SAFE

As you grow up, there are lots of changes to cope with in your life. Apart from the changes going on with your body and feelings, becoming an adult means taking responsibility for your own actions and learning to make smart choices and decisions. This is especially important if you find yourself in a tricky situation, and need a way of dealing with it.

Sometimes friends or other people might try to put pressure on you to do things you don't like, are too young to do, or that are dangerous or unhealthy. This could be things like persuading you to miss school or stay out late. But it could also be trying to force you to smoke or drink alcohol, or touching you when you don't want them to. Don't forget, whatever happens, you always have the right to be safe and secure. You also have the right to say "No", even though this can be hard to do. Say it loud and clear, and you'll soon get the message across.

FACTFILE: BEING BULLIED

- Bullying happens in lots of different ways. You might get teased, pushed, kicked or called names. Someone might say things that frighten or threaten you. A bully might try to grab your things or turn your friends against you.
- Bullying can happen to anyone. It doesn't matter how old, or young, you are. And it can happen anywhere — at school, on the way to or from school, at home, while playing sports, at a youth club, and even by text or online. About two-thirds of young people say they've been bullied at some time.

- Bullies often pick on people they know they can upset easily. This gives them a feeling of power. Some bullies don't even realize they're doing it. They think it's funny to tease someone, and don't reckon it does any harm. But some bullies deliberately set out to make people miserable. They don't care about their feelings.

- Whatever happens, bullying is never okay. If you're being bullied, don't suffer alone. Tell an adult what's happening. They'll help to stop the bullying. Remember, it is not your fault. It's the bully who has the problem, not you.
- As much as you can, avoid being in the same place as the bully. Even if it means taking a different route to school. Walk to school and back with a friend, and stay with them at lunchtime or during break.

- If you do come across the bully, try ignoring them. If they say anything, pretend you haven't heard them, then walk away. Bullies want to see how you react, and if you act as if you couldn't care less, they might just stop picking on you.
- If you see someone else being bullied, don't just stand by and watch. Tell the bully to stop, or, if you feel uncomfortable doing that, go and talk to an adult.

Just as no one should ever try to bully you, you should never bully other people. It isn't clever and it isn't smart. Everyone deserves to be treated fairly and with respect. It's never okay to pick on someone because they look different than you, for example, or come from a different culture or background. Learning to accept other people is an important part of growing up.

CYBER SAFETY

The Internet is the place where you talk to old friends, meet new friends, share each other's photos, go shopping, listen to music and watch films. It connects you to millions of other people and places all over the world. But this can also make it easier for strangers to find out about you, perhaps with the idea of harming or taking advantage of you. So it's really important to know how to surf safely and have fun at the same time. Here are some top tips for staying safe and smart online:

* If you're setting up a profile on a social networking site or joining a chat room, make up a false name. Don't use your real one.
* Don't give away personal details about yourself, friends or family, such as your address, phone number or school. Remember, you don't always know who you're talking to.
* Set your security settings so that only your chosen friends can see your profile. Don't add anyone you don't know to your friends' list.
* Be very, very careful about any pictures you post. You never know who might see them. Don't post anything you wouldn't want your parents or teachers to see. To be on the safe side, use a photo of your favorite pet or celeb instead.

* If you're writing a blog, be careful not to give away too many details about you or your life. The same goes if you're posting about something like a party. Don't give the address.

* Don't arrange to meet up with anyone you talk to online. Some people lie and may not be who they say they are.

* Don't believe everything you read on the Web. There are good and bad websites.

Smart Girl Talk

Cyberbullying is when people send nasty or threatening messages online or by mobile phone. Not only is it really upsetting, it's also against the law. If it happens to you, don't reply to any messages or texts but save them and show them to an adult. To be safe, only give your mobile number to friends and people you trust, and keep your online passwords secret.

TALKING ABOUT IT

And finally, if you ever find yourself in a situation you can't handle, there are plenty of people you can go to for help. If you don't feel you can talk to your friends or family, try a teacher, school counsellor, nurse or doctor, or someone at your local church or youth club. Don't worry – anything you tell them stays strictly between you and them. But remember, no one has the right to ask you to keep something secret if it hurts you, or puts you at risk. Don't keep things bottled up if they're making you unhappy or anxious. Tell someone you can trust.

EPILOGUE

Congratulations! You've survived the puberty roller coaster with all of its ups and downs. And it has been an exciting, and rocky, ride. You've got brand-new breasts and have been out shopping for bras. You've coped with starting your periods and getting pimples. You've grown hair in places where you didn't have hair before, and you're nearly as tall as your mom. You've fallen out with your friends, made up with your friends, and fallen out with them all over again. And if that's not enough, you've had the BIGGEST crush on the best-looking boy in your class, and he hasn't even noticed you. Still, you haven't turned into an alien. In fact, you're feeling fabulous — most of the time. Of course, puberty's not over yet but you're getting used to all the changes, and the not-so-great parts won't last for ever. No one ever went through puberty without having lows as well as highs. It won't be long before you're looking back at this time in your life, and wondering what all the fuss was about. After all, if you're reading this guide, you're already pretty smart.

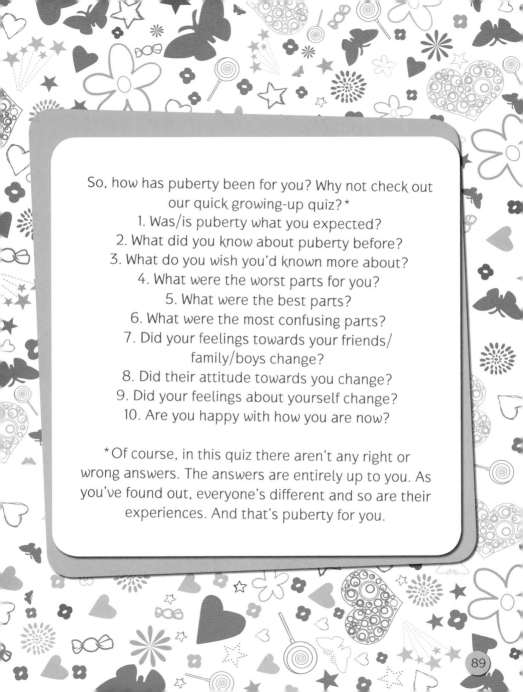

So, how has puberty been for you? Why not check out our quick growing-up quiz?*

1. Was/is puberty what you expected?
2. What did you know about puberty before?
3. What do you wish you'd known more about?
4. What were the worst parts for you?
5. What were the best parts?
6. What were the most confusing parts?
7. Did your feelings towards your friends/family/boys change?
8. Did their attitude towards you change?
9. Did your feelings about yourself change?
10. Are you happy with how you are now?

*Of course, in this quiz there aren't any right or wrong answers. The answers are entirely up to you. As you've found out, everyone's different and so are their experiences. And that's puberty for you.

GLOSSARY

Bacteria Microscopic living things that can be helpful or harmful.

Condoms Rubbery covers than fit on to a man's penis during sex. They stop sperm entering a woman's vagina and also stop some sexual diseases from spreading.

Contraceptives Devices, such as condoms, or drugs, such as the pill, that prevent a woman from getting pregnant.

Eating disorder An illness, such as anorexia or bulimia, caused when people have a problem with food and eating that takes over their lives.

Eggs Cells made in a woman's ovaries. Also called ova.

Fertilized When male sperm cells join with a female egg so that a baby starts growing.

Flossing Using a thin piece of tape, or special brush, to clean between your teeth.

Genes Special codes in your body cells that are passed on to you by your parents. They control your hair and eye color, whether you are tall or short, and so on.

Genitals The sex organs on the outside of your body.

Glands Organs in your body that make chemicals, for example, your sweat glands.

Groin The area of the body where your legs join your abdomen (trunk).

Hormones Powerful chemicals made in organs called glands. Hormones travel through your bloodstream and affect different parts of your body.

Menopause The time when a woman's ovaries stop making eggs and her periods stop happening.

Menstrual cycle The number of days from the start of one period to the beginning of the next period.

Moisturizer A cream that you put on your skin to keep it soft and supple.

Oestrogen A type of female sex hormone.

Ovaries A woman's sex organs that make eggs and female sex hormones. You have two inside your body, one of either side of your uterus (womb) in your lower abdomen.

Ovulation When, each month, an egg travels out of one of your ovaries and down into your uterus.

Penis A man's sex organ that fits inside a woman's vagina during sex.

Period pains Aching cramps that you might feel before and during your period.

Periods A few days of bleeding from your vagina that happen every month if the eggs you make are not fertilized.

Plaque A film of food and bacteria that sticks to your teeth and can cause holes in your teeth and lead to gum problems.

Pregnant When a woman has a baby growing inside her uterus (womb). Pregnancy lasts for about 40 weeks.

Pre-menstrual syndrome (PMS, for short) Feeling tired, bloated and irritable in the days before your period starts.

Progesterone A type of female sex hormone.

Pubic hair Short, wiry hair that grows around the sex organs on the outside of your body.

Sanitary towels Rectangular pads of asborbent material that soak up blood during your periods. You wear them inside your pants.

Sex When a man's penis fits inside a woman's vagina. Also called sexual intercourse.

Sex organs The parts of the body that are used to make babies (reproduction). Also known as reproductive organs.

Sperm A male sex cell that is made in the testicles. If it joins with a female egg, it can grow into a baby.

Tampons Small rolls of absorbent material that soak up blood during your periods. You wear one inside your vagina.

Testicles A man's sex organs that make sperm and male sex hormones, such as testosterone.

Testosterone A type of male sex hormone.

Thrush An infection of your vagina that can make it smelly and itchy.

Toxic shock syndrome A rare but serious illness that can be caused by leaving a tampon inside you for too long. (TSS, for short.)

Uterus A muscular, pear-shaped organ in your body where a baby grows. It stretches as the baby gets bigger. Also called your womb.

Vagina A stretchy tube leading from your uterus to the outside of your body.

Vaginal discharge A normally clear or milky fluid that comes out of your vagina and helps to keep it healthy.

NOTES

INDEX